St. Louis Community College

Forest Park
Florissant Valley
Meramec

Instructional Resources
St. Louis, Missouri

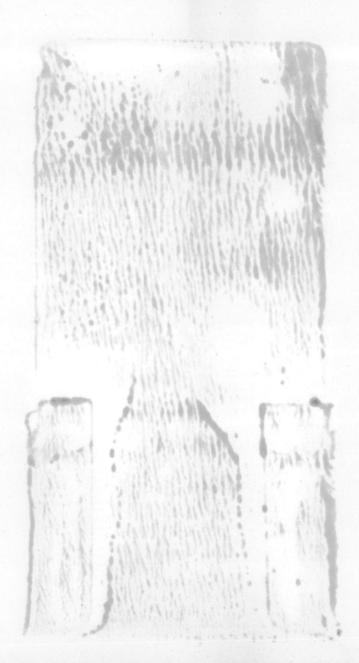

SILK SCREEN PRINTING FOR THE ARTIST

SILK SCREEN PRINTING FOR THE ARTIST

ROGER MARSH

NEW YORK / TRANSATLANTIC ARTS INC / 1968

First American Edition published by
Transatlantic Arts Inc., 1968
565 Fifth Avenue,
New York, NY 10017

MADE AND PRINTED IN THE UNITED KINGDOM
(GB) SBN 85458-110/3c

CONTENTS

PREFACE

Basically screen printing is only a step further than stencilling; it is a simple yet ingenious way of holding a stencil design together while ink is being forced passed onto paper. The printing is done through a screen which consists of a frame with a mesh material stretched over it. Parts of the mesh are blocked out with a stencil, and the screen is placed over the area to be printed. Ink is then pulled across the mesh with a squeegee and the ink passes through the open parts of the mesh to print onto the area underneath.

The medium of silk screen printing is more than a method of graphic reproduction, it is a means by which the artist can transform his ideas into visual images.

The aim of this book is to present the medium of silk screen printing to the artist, to reveal the potential, and to show clearly what the medium can offer. All the information is basic and deals directly with the producing of images, with the emphasis upon experiment and investigation.

The book is divided into four sections, each section is presented to the reader as an introduction to various areas for further study. Prints and illustrations have been chosen carefully for their aptness in amplifying various aspects of the text.

I gratefully acknowledge the kindness of the artists who have given me permission to reproduce their work.

I wish also to thank my family for help and support in the preparation of this book.

Roger Marsh

INTRODUCTION

Stencilling in its simplest form is the covering of a surface with a thin impervious material, paper, plastic etc., in which openings have been cut, revealing parts of the surface underneath. Paint, ink or dye is dabbed through the open parts, thus when the stencil is removed, the shapes of the cut areas are printed onto the surface underneath.

The hand prints on the walls of the Gargas Caves are amongst the earliest examples of stencilling. These prints were produced by placing the hand on the wall of the cave, and pigment blown from the mouth or down through a tube onto the area left uucovered by the hand. The hand was then removed to reveal the stencilled print.

The Egyptians and the Greeks probably made use of stencilling to print upon their pots, fabrics, buildings etc., and it is recorded that children of Roman times were introduced to letters of their alphabet by drawing them through lettered cut stencils. In the Far East the early Chinese and Japanese had mastered the art of stencilling, as can be seen in the prints of Buddhas in the Tun-Huang caves, and on Japanese ceremonial robes.

For centuries, the stencil was used for colouring woodcuts, and laying areas of colour upon wallpaper, fabrics, buildings and also furniture.

With stencilling giving such an early appearance (Gargas 15,000–10,000 B.C.; Chinese fourth century A.D.) it is surprising that no real development was made until the late seventeenth and early eighteenth centuries.

Although intricate designs can be cut in a stencil, there are limitations imposed by the fact that the stencil must hold together. All 'floating' areas must be attached to the body of the stencil by 'bridges'; therefore when it is printed, the 'bridges' have to be accepted as part of the design. This limitation was overcome by Japanese stencil cutters by attaching hair to the floating areas in a web-like fashion, thus holding the design together, the hair being fine enough to be barely visible when the image was printed. The hair was often stretched across a frame in a grid system and the stencil attached to it. This being the forerunner of silk screen printing as it is known to-day.

From the basic principle of hair being stretched across a frame, and a stencil attached to the hair, further research and experiment was carried out to develop the process.

Experiments with silk to hold the stencil, were carried out in Europe in the 1870s and later developed in England. It is recorded that in 1907 a patent was taken out, covering the use of a mesh screen to hold a stencil, the use of a squeegee was not included; ink had to be forced through the screen with a stiff brush.

Yet, although the process had its roots in the Far East, England and other parts of Europe, it was the Americans that realised silk screen printing had a commercial value, and if further developed could successfully compete with the existing processes. This development took place, and as soon as the possibilities were evident, silk screen printing units soon sprang up, and today these have developed into a highly mechanised and thriving industry.

Throughout the development of silk screen printing the artist appeared to be reluctant to accept the process as a medium to be exploited. Perhaps it was the association the medium had with 'commercial art', or it could have been that no artist had given it the prestige which etching and lithography had acquired, but whatever the reasons, there is a strong move today towards a full acceptance; in fact the artist is keen to investigate, not only silk screen printing, but almost any process from which an image can be obtained.

This book presents silk screen printing as an autographic process. Once the technical aspects have been mastered, the way lies open to further investigation into using the principles and suggestions as a point of departure for continued study.

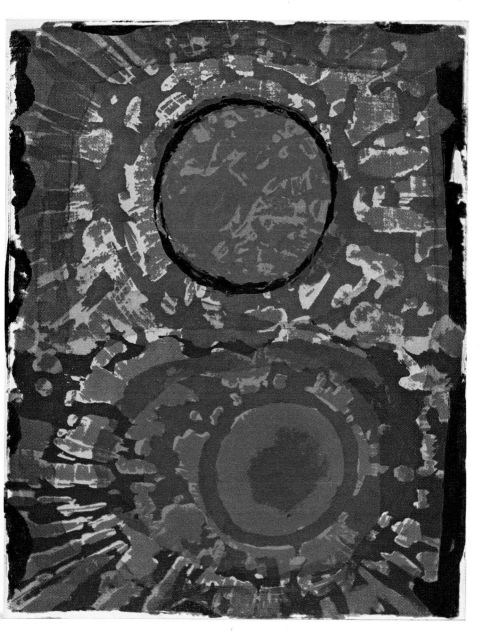

PLATE I. *The Elements* by Roger Marsh. This print was produced from the nucleus of an idea, and was developed by working directly upon the mesh, forming the print with each successive printing. Two stencil methods were employed in the formation of the image: the glue and the paper methods (*see* pages 19 and 21)

CHAPTER ONE

THE PRINTING UNIT

THE FRAME

The printing unit comprises of a frame over which is stretched a mesh material in readiness to accept a stencil. The frame is attached to a baseboard which provides the printing area.

The size of the frame is determined by the scale at which the printmaker works. The measurements given will make a frame 1 foot 6 inches by 2 feet, this size will be suitable for average size prints. The following are materials required to make the frame.

1 length of soft wood; 8 feet of 2 inches by 1 inch, seasoned and straight.

1 length of wood; 1 foot by $\frac{1}{2}$ inch by $\frac{1}{2}$ inch (to make the support Fig. 9).

4 right-angle brackets, flat type with screws.

1, one-inch screw with washer.

Medium sandpaper.

Glue.

Panel pins.

These can easily be acquired at low cost from any timber shop. For joining the corners to make the frame, Fig. 1; place glue on the

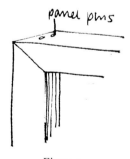

panel pins

Figure 1

joints, and with the aid of a piece of string, Fig. 2, hold the frame in position. While the glue is setting, lay the frame down on a flat surface and place weights on each of the corners, Fig. 3. This will   74

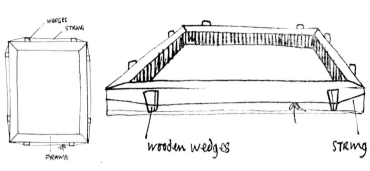

Figure 2

make sure that the frame will be flat. When the glue has set hard, the joints can be secured with panel pins or right-angle brackets. Alternatively methods for joining the corners can be seen in Figs. 4

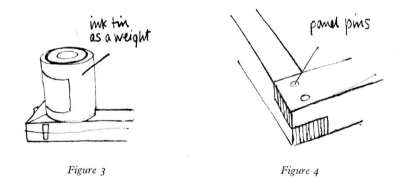

Figure 3   *Figure 4*

and 5. These will have to be constructed with the aid of a vice, as the string method is only practical with the joint in Fig. 1. The more skilled can use dove-tail or mortice and tenon joints.

It is important that the frame be rigid, and that it can lay flat. Now decide which is to be the underside of the frame and bevel its outside edges to about one eighth radius, Fig. 6. The reason for this
75   is to prevent tearing the mesh as it is being stretched over the frame. Finish off the job by removing all rough edges with a medium sand-
76   paper.

The frame sometime during its usage will be placed in water, it is wise therefore to paint the frame with a coat of shellac, if using oil based inks, or primed and painted with household paint if cellulose ink is used. This will make it waterproof and prevent distortion.

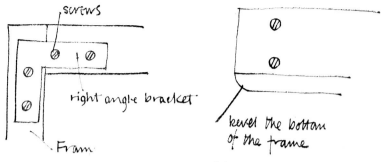

Figures 5 and 6

THE BASEBOARD

The baseboard holds the frame and forms the printing surface.*
Materials required for the baseboard
2 foot by 2 foot 6 inches of ½ inch plywood.
2 hinges (partable type) with screws.
The plywood must be perfectly flat, anything which spoils the smoothness of the surface must be sanded down.
Place the frame in a central position of the plywood.
Screw the hinges to the short side of the screen, and down to the plywood base, Fig. 7. The partable type hinges used allow the frame

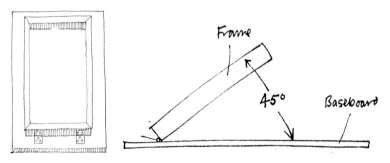

Figures 7 and 8

*The baseboard is for use where there is no permanent printing area. For example, if the printmaker works on a table top which is also used for designing, then the printing unit will have to be made portable. But if he is fortunate in having an area which is used for no other purpose than printing, then no baseboard is necessary. The table or bench top will have to be prepared in the same way as the baseboard, the hinges will be screwed along one side of the table, and should be in a position to accept any other screen.

to be removed off the base quite simply. The frame should be able to swing from the level of the baseboard to an upright position, Fig. 8. A support will be needed to hold the frame in a raised position of 45°. This can be done as in Fig. 9.

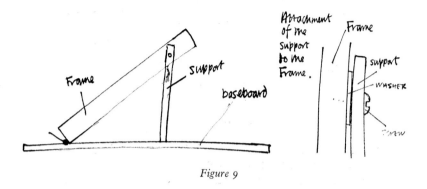

Figure 9

An alternative suggestion for attaching the frame to the baseboard can be seen in Fig. 10. This method is ideal for printing on thick materials.

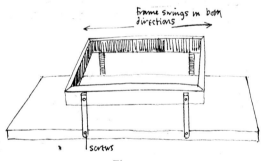

Figure 10

These methods of hinging the frame to the baseboard, and holding it in a raised position have proved themselves to be the simplest and most practical. If they do not fulfil your particular requirements, other more ingenious methods can be invented. When the frame is attached to the baseboard pencil marks can be drawn around the top two corners on to the baseboard (furthest away from the hinges). These lines will act as register guides to check that when the screen is raised it will be lowered into the same position each time.

The Mesh. The next operation is to stretch a mesh material over the frame. The selection of the mesh depends largely upon what demands are to be made.

Not so long ago, silk bolting cloth and cotton organdie were the only mesh materials suitable for screen printing. Silk became synonymous with the medium, and thus has been termed as silk screen printing, a term which is applied to this day, although not strictly correct.

Silk and cotton are still the most widely used of all the meshes, although there are many other mesh materials available to be used; for example, nylon, rayon, terylene, stainless steel, phosphor-bronze and copper gauze. Experiments with these materials should be carried out to find the limitations and possibilities of each material.

Silk. The best silk is manufactured in Switzerland and although perhaps very expensive, can be proven, over a period of time, to be more economical than the cheaper makes. Silk is hygroscopic and therefore a certain amount of stretching or shrinking may be noticed when it is positioned on the screen. This movement of the silk does not usually affect registration. A constant temperature in the work-room will keep distortion to a minimum.

The life of silk, can, with careful handling be expected to last through scores of stencils and many editions. This is remarkable when considering the mesh will be washed with water, turpentine substitute or cellulose solvent time and time again; heated with an iron, and have the squeegee scraped over it thousands of times.

The strength of silk is not only in itself but in the way it has been woven. The threads running across the width (referred to as the weft) are interlocked with the threads running the length of the material (the warp). A silk with a plain weave, although not as strong as the interlock is available and is ideal for printing with photographic stencils.

Hardwearing as it is, it will seldom stand a gash from a sharp edge. If this does occur, and the damage is only a small cut not falling in an open area of the stencil to be used, it can be patched by attaching pieces of gum strip slightly larger than the cut. These should be gummed on both sides of the mesh. If oil-based inks are to be used for printing, the patch can be painted with shellac to give it added strength, but if cellulose inks are to be used, leave the patch unpainted. For the cellulose will soften shellac, and if used, can be dragged off the patch by the squeegee, and be deposited in the mesh, thus blocking it. The patch can survive through a few stencils but should only be regarded as a temporary measure.

When purchasing silk there is a standard code relating to various qualities and grades. The quality and weight of silk is governed by the thickness of the threads, and is marked by an x. The number of mesh openings and fineness is called the grade, this being represented by numbers. A low number denotes a coarse mesh, while a high number relates to a finer one. The quality of silk most generally used by printmakers is xx and the grade chosen is determined by the type of print to be undertaken, be it heavily textured or containing intricate detail. As a guide: number 8 for coarse work and number 14 for fine work. These thus would read as 8xx and 14xx.

Cotton Organdie. Cotton organdie is ideally suited to the more coarser and heavily textured prints. It is cheap to buy, however it has a limited life and is restricted in its uses.

The mesh of cotton organdie is not interlocked and corresponds in grade to that in coarse silk. It has a very uneven weave and tears easily. The fibres of the mesh will, after a few printing sessions, begin to part and can clog the mesh. It is also easily affected by humidity which can make even simple registration difficult. Therefore water and water-based stencils should be avoided.

Stretching Procedure. Having decided which mesh is to be used, it has to be stretched over the frame as taut as possible. To do this

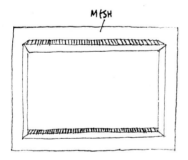

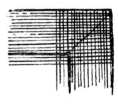

Figure 11   *Figure 12*

the mesh should be cut about 2 inches larger than the frame (Fig. 11) the weft and the warp being in line with the frame (Fig. 12). The best way of stretching the mesh is found only through experience, for suggestions Figs. 13, and 14, the numbers indicate the order in

which the mesh is stapled or tacked to the frame. In Fig. 13 it will
be noticed that the route taken is from top to bottom, then from side

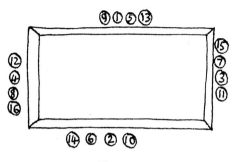

Figure 13

to side, this is then repeated moving each time out towards the
corners. The route taken in Fig. 14 is from A to B, A to C, B to D
and then in from the corners of C and D.

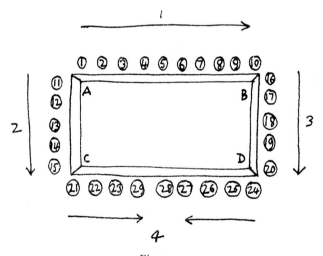

Figure 14

During the stretching the frame should occasionally be held up
towards the light so that ripples or creases can be seen.

When the screen has been stretched the corners should be folded
as in Fig. 15 and a safety margin applied around the edges of the
screen, Fig. 16, both inside and out. Gum strip or masking tape
can be used. If gum strip is used, it should be painted with shellac

13

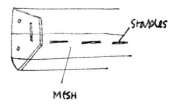

MESH

Figure 15

to make it waterproof; that is of course if cellulose inks are not to be used, for the same reason given in dealing with a patch. The safety margin as the name implies is to allow a safety area for the ink during printing—see printing operation page 41. It also has a dual role of stopping ink from creeping between the frame and the

UNDERSIDE OF FRAME

MASKING TAPE

Figure 16a

mesh where it is difficult to remove and where it would eventually rot the mesh; and also to allow for easy scooping up of ink at the edges and sides after printing. The screen is now ready to receive the stencil.

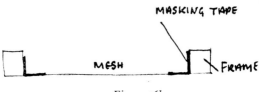

MASKING TAPE

MESH FRAME

Figure 16b

14

PLATE II. *The Branches* by Roger Marsh. In contrast to the way the print *The Elements* (plate I) was formed, this print began with a full colour layout. Photographic stencils were employed to reproduce the image (*see* page 29)

The squeegee is the tool which is used to pull the ink from one side of the screen to the other. It must be able to fit inside the frame, leaving a clearance of about ½ inch on either side of the squeegee, Fig. 17.

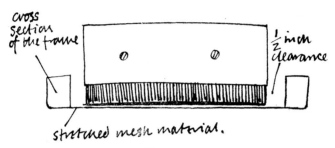

Figure 17

The squeegee consists of a strip of rubber gripped in a wooden handle. The rubber in the squeegee can be genuine rubber or synthetic; black or white, hard or soft. It can be attached permanently into the handle, or designed so that it can be interchangeable with other squeegee rubber blades. Blades can be bevelled at various angles to suit printing upon different materials.

There are so many personal preferences involved which govern the design of a squeegee, that no one squeegee can be made which can perform to the demands of every printmaker.

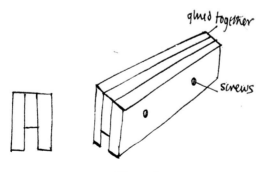

Figure 18

The details given below will produce a squeegee to suit general needs.

Materials required to make a squeegee to fit the frame on page 7:

C

2 lengths of wood 1 foot 5 inches of 4 inches by $\frac{3}{8}$.
1 length of wood 1 foot 5 inches of 4 inches by $\frac{3}{8}$.
1 strip of rubber 1 foot 5 inches of 2 inches by $\frac{3}{8}$.
Glue.
$\frac{1}{2}$ inch screws.

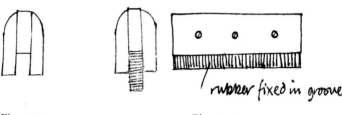

rubber fixed in groove

Figure 19   Figure 20

The wood lengths can be glued and screwed together; for construction see Fig. 18. Round off the top edges, Fig. 19 and sandpaper any rough projections.

The length of rubber can be slipped along the groove and secured in position by glue, Fig. 20.

Test that the base of the rubber is straight by placing it on a flat surface, Fig. 21.

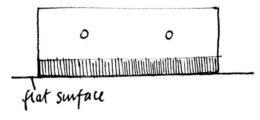

flat surface

Figure 21

The rubber will tend to round off with use, when this happens it can be made sharp again by rubbing it on a sanding block. This can easily be made by glueing a strip of sandpaper along a length of wood, the squeegee is then pushed along the sandpaper until the roundness is replaced by a sharp edge.

Materials required for a sanding block:

1 length of wood 3 feet by 4 inches.

1 strip of sandpaper 3 feet by 3 inches.

(The strip can be made from short lengths of sandpaper).

CHAPTER TWO

STENCILS

THE IMAGE

The process of silk screen printing is more than a method of graphic reproduction, it is a means by which the artist can transform his ideas into visual images, and it can also have a direct bearing upon the formation of the original ideas. The relationship between the artist and this medium can reach an understanding and sensitivity that ideas are thought of in terms of the medium; the idea being the beginning of the print, although still in the mind of the artist.

The idea can emerge in various ways, how it does so is an entirely personal matter between the artist and his method of working.

He can prepare a full colour design of the intended print, and separate all the colours ready to make the stencils; in contrast a simple sketch can be used, or even no guide at all, working spontaneously from one print to another, or perhaps a combination of various methods. Whatever method is chosen to make the idea visually tangible, stencils have to be prepared in readiness for printing.

Transfer of image to a stencil. Working with a layout

The designing of a full colour layout involves the working out of the intended print to its logical conclusions. Any medium can be used to achieve this, for example with paint, coloured papers, coloured ink, crayons etc.: the layout should be scaled to the size of the intended print. When the layout is complete, each colour has to be separated and a stencil made of each one. As a guide the largest and lightest area can be chosen first.

The Procedure. When the layout is complete the sequence in which each colour will be printed has to be decided. When this has been concluded, the colours in the layout have to be separated.

The procedure of doing this varies slightly with each stencil method used.

Paper stencils

1. A tracing is made of the layout, drawing around the boundary of each colour. This is the master copy.

2. The master copy is placed on top of the paper selected to be the stencil with a piece of carbon tissue in between. The colour selected to be printed first is traced off the master copy on to the paper stencil. See paper stencils, page 19. This done, the same procedure is repeated consecutively with each colour in turn.

3. The stencils now have to be cut, this can be done with a sharp thin bladed knife. The stencils should be cut slightly larger than the guide line shows. This will allow for the colours overlapping in printing and give accurate registration leaving no white lines between the colours.

Hand Drawn Stencils. There is no need to make a master copy with hand drawn stencils.

1. A prepared screen is positioned over the top of the layout.

2. Guide lines are made around the selected colour on to the mesh with a pencil or ball point pen.

3. The layout can be removed and the stencil painted on to the screen.

4. This procedure is repeated with each colour.

Film Stencils. See film stencils, method of procedure, page 26.

Photographic Stencils. See photographic stencils, method of procedure, page 30.

With the printing of a previously designed layout there will almost certainly be 'developments or happenings' beneficial to the print, unforeseen during the designing stage. These qualities should be recognised as being contributive to the print, though they can cause frustration to the inexperienced who does not wish to depart from the original idea. Only through experience will the printmaker be able to harness all the qualities revealed during the printing operation and still be able to conclude the original idea.

Transfer of image to a stencil. Working without a layout

As previously mentioned it is not essential to have a completed layout. The artist can work directly with the stencils upon the screen, formulating his ideas, anticipating the growth of the image with each printing. This way of working allows for more scope with images to be developed. A single set of prints can be developed, or an 'additive' method can be employed.

Additive Method. After the first images have been printed, the second stencil is completed, and is printed upon the first prints, and also printed as a first colour upon fresh paper. A third stencil is made, printed upon the first prints, with the second colour upon them; and also on to the second colour now as the first colour; then printing the third colour as a first colour upon fresh paper.

Although only three stencils have been used, there are already three separate developments taking place, each with a growth of its own. The only limit to the additive method is that imposed by the printmaker.

It has also been mentioned that a combination of various methods can be operated. What is referred to is the practise of working out planned layouts to be further developed after many prints have already been produced; or the branching out at a tangent during the process of printing a designed layout.

Stencils. The function of the stencil is to block out parts of the mesh while ink is being forced, through the parts left open, onto paper previously placed underneath, thus producing the print.

Stencils can take many forms, the main ones being paper, water-based glue, greasy ink or chalk, film stencils and photographic stencils.

PAPER STENCILS

Paper stencils are used mainly for printing large areas of colour and simple designs. Only simple shapes should be cut, as intricate designs will not hold together, unless the stencil is cut with such ingenuity that intricate designs will not fall to pieces.

Ingenious use, or rather misuse of paper has proved, however, that paper stencils are not limited purely to the functions forementioned. Prints can be made from papers of different thicknesses, used on the screen together; or paper used after being burnt in areas, abrased over textured surfaces, torn or cut.

The paper used for the stencil in the printing of simple cut-out shapes, should be thin, yet strong and non-absorbent. Transparent or semi-transparent paper is a good choice for a stencil, for if a layout is used, the colour needed to be cut can be traced directly off the layout, without the use of a master copy. Paper can be strengthened by wiping both sides with a piece of rag charged with shellac, and should be used only with oil-based inks, see page 37. Stiff grease proof paper is widely used, and even newsprint. Newsprint will only suffice for very short runs. If longer runs are required, then a second or third duplicate stencil should be cut, for when the first stencil begins to break up duplicate stencils can be cut by placing the paper stencils as one, and cutting them together.

All types of paper should be investigated. For example absorbent papers are not normally found suitable, yet during experiments I have found that where ink begins to seep through the paper (which a non-absorbent paper would prevent) an image can, with careful squeegee handling, be printed from the leakage consistently for a number of prints.

Materials required:
Paper for the stencil.
Thin bladed cutting knife.
Masking tape (for register marks).
Screen and base board.
Newsprint.

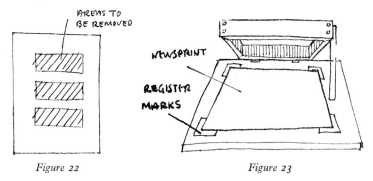

Figure 22   Figure 23

Method of Procedure

1. Cut out parts of the stencil where ink is to pass, Fig. 22.
2. A sheet of newsprint, the same size as the paper to be used for printing the edition, is placed on the printing area (base-

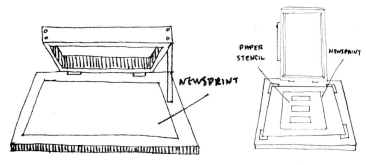

Figure 24   Figure 25

board), Fig. 23, and register marks placed at the corners of the newsprint, Fig. 24, also see registration, page 40.

3. The cut stencil is placed on top of the newsprint, Fig. 25. If there are any detached pieces of stencil (islands) care must be exercised in placing them in the correct position relative to the rest of the stencil.

4. Lower the screen down to the printing position. Check that when the screen is lowered it falls directly over the stencil. To safeguard any movement, a water-based glue can be dabbed through the mesh at various key points on to the stencil, holding it in position. Any 'islands' should be secured. Allow the glue to dry. The stencil is now ready for printing; see printing operation, page 41.

5. With the first printing, ink will be forced through the mesh, attaching the paper stencil to the mesh. The ink passing through the open parts of the mesh will be deposited on to the newsprint underneath.

6. Raise the screen, and with care, remove the printed newsprint, making sure that the paper stencil remains attached to the screen.

HAND DRAWN STENCILS

Applying the drawing directly upon the mesh is termed Serigraphy, derived from the Latin *sericus*—silk, and the Greek *graphia*—drawing. The term today however has a larger application, relating to the artists' use of the medium of silk screen printing. Two basic procedures exist with drawing directly upon the mesh, that of using glue, and that of using greasy ink (tusche). The application of glue will produce a negative print, for where the glue is painted onto the mesh it will be left as white when printed. It is possible to get a positive effect by printing onto a colour. The colour showing through the negative areas will read as positive. When grease is applied to the mesh the print will be produced as a positive, i.e. where the grease was applied will later become the open areas of the mesh.

The Glue Method

Glue is used to draw the design upon the screen thus blocking out parts of the mesh, and becoming the stencil. The glue used is water-based and must be easily solvent to water. Glue which is quite suitable to use is that mixed up from glue-size (instructions supplied). It should be mixed to a medium strength. During mixing, a small amount of white or black poster paint should be added so that the glue-size can be seen as it is painted onto the screen. If a water-based glue is to be bought, check that it is not of a type that becomes waterproof when it has dried. Experience is the only guide to the correct working strength to mix the glue, if it is too thin it will not block the mesh properly, printing with small pinholes. If it is too thick, application of the glue onto the mesh will be found most difficult, and may not hold during printing. Test dabs should be made on the safe part of the mesh. Allow to dry and check that no pinholes are present; if they are, the glue can be thickened slightly. The glue can be applied to the mesh in various ways. The brush is the most widely used tool, although strips of card, feathers, folded paper and even fingers make suitable applicants. Any material with a strong textured surface can be used; coat the textured surface with glue, then press it onto the mesh, transferring the glue. Great care should be taken that the textured surface does not damage the mesh. It is also possible to apply the glue to a damp screen, thinning the glue in varying degrees, which will print as a very soft tone, or blowing onto the wet glue, producing pinholes to soften the sharp edges.

Materials required:
    Water-based glue.
    Poster paint.
    Materials and tools to apply the glue.
    Rag.
    Water for erasing.

Method of Procedure:
    1. Draw the design upon the screen using a water-based glue. Corrections can be made by removing glue with water applied carefully with a piece of rag onto the area to be erased. To

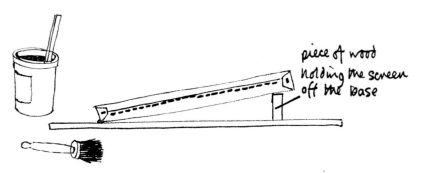

Figure 26a

PLATE III. *Still Life* by George Todd. The exhibits show quite clearly a plasticity and freedom wherein lie the true sympathetic aspects of screen printing which will lend themselves fully to the demands of the artist

DESIGN PAINTED FREELY ON TO THE SCREEN

MESH

STRIP OF WOOD HOLDING
THE SCREEN OFF THE BASE

Figure 26b

guard against the glue sticking the mesh to the baseboard, work with the frame raised two or three inches, Fig. 26. If working with a layout see transfer of image to a stencil, page 17.
2. When the drawing on the screen has been completed, allow time for the glue to set. The screen is now ready for printing—see printing operation, page 41.
3. The result is a negative print.

The Grease Method

The design is drawn onto the screen with lithographer's ink, or with greasy crayon (known as tusche in America). As with the glue method the greasy ink can be applied to the mesh with brush, card or feather, etc., whereas the crayon is drawn directly. Almost any greasy crayon is suitable providing it can be washed out of the mesh with turpentine. Crayon must be applied with a certain amount of pressure or it will not be deposited sufficiently upon the mesh, a staining can give the effect that the mesh is blocked. Textured materials can be placed beneath the mesh, and with a greasy crayon take a rubbing upon the mesh taking care not to damage the mesh. The use of grease may at first be found to be a little clumsy but the more it is used the easier this method will become.

Method of Procedure:

    1. The design is drawn upon the mesh with a lithographic ink or crayon. Work with the screen raised, Fig. 26.

    2. When drawing is complete allow time to dry.

    3. Mix up an amount of water-based glue slightly thinner than that mixed for the glue method. With the screen still raised, place an amount of glue enough to cover the mesh in the safety margin at the bottom of the screen.

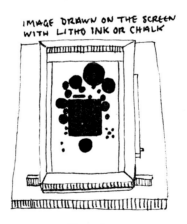

Figure 27

    4. With the squeegee or a straight-edged piece of card pull the glue to the top of the screen, Fig. 27. The glue should have blocked all the undrawn parts of the mesh not passing or running through the underside, Fig. 28.

5. Remove all excess glue from the top and sides of the screen and allow to dry. As a safety measure the process can be repeated again to make certain that all the mesh is blocked.

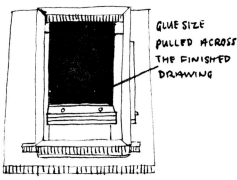

GLUE SIZE PULLED ACROSS THE FINISHED DRAWING

Figure 28

6. Place a few sheets of newsprint under the frame, lowering it down flat. Apply turpentine or turpentine substitute to the mesh and with a piece of rag carefully wash out the greasy drawing, Fig. 29. The grease should be persuaded, not scrubbed out of the mesh, rough treatment will result in a breakdown of the glue, or worse, damage to the mesh. Stubborn patches of

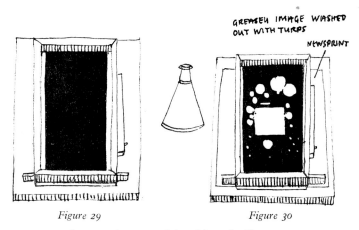

GREASEY IMAGE WASHED OUT WITH TURPS

NEWSPRINT

Figure 29   Figure 30

grease can be eased away with a blunt knife.

7. Hold the mesh up to the light and check that the grease has been removed, also check that the glue stencil has not been weakened. If any holes are seen they can be filled with glue.

8. The stencil is now ready for printing, see printing operation, page 41. The result will be a positive print. With both these methods the stencil can be removed from the screen by washing out the glue with warm water.

FILM STENCILS

The use of a film stencil will produce when printed basically the same quality as a paper stencil. The advantage a film stencil has is that accurate and intricate shapes can be cut without the stencil falling to pieces, and also it is capable of being used for long runs.

There are many kinds of film stencils available. I find the most suitable and widely used to be 'Profilm', 'Bluefilm' and 'Greenfilm'. Profilm is for use with oil-based inks and consists of a shellac film, bonded to tissue paper, this being temporarily attached by a paraffin wax to a backing sheet. With the introduction of cellulose inks another film had to be found as shellac is affected by cellulose solvents. Hence Bluefilm. This is made in the same way as Profilm but the tissue is coated with fish glue instead of shellac. Greenfilm was introduced to give better adhesion to Nylon, Terylene, etc. and metallic meshes.

The design is cut out of the film (the shapes to be printed) and removed from the backing sheet. The film remaining upon the backing sheet is ironed into the mesh, and the backing sheet carefully removed, leaving the film attached. Both these films are semi-transparent and can be laid over the finished layout and various areas can be cut. If, however, yellow colours are used in the layout, they can be very difficult to see when cutting with Profilm. The same applies to Bluefilm and Greenfilm with green-blue colours. To overcome this, a master tracing can be made and placed under the film instead of the layout.

Method of Procedure:

    1. Place a sheet of the stencil, film side uppermost over the top of the finished layout, Fig. 31. The film should be cut about 2 inches larger.

    2. With a sharp knife cut out the parts of the design where ink is intended to pass, that is, cut through the film to the backing sheet, not through it for it is the backing sheet which holds the design together. Peel off the film as each part of the design is cut out, Fig. 32. It is advisable to place a small piece of paper between the hand that is cutting the film, and the film itself, for moisture from the hand can transfer grease upon the film, and with Bluefilm and Greenfilm soften the glue.

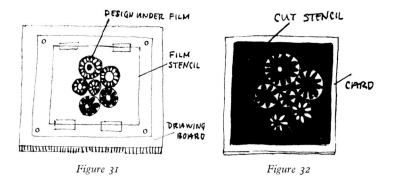

Figure 31   Figure 32

3. When the design is finally cut out, place the film stencil on to a piece of card, film side uppermost and arrange it under the screen, Fig. 33. If Bluefilm or Greenfilm is used the mesh should be dampened before the film is placed under the screen. The card will make the mesh taut (the mesh must be free from grease)* giving perfect contact. Then lay a piece of newsprint inside the frame.

SIDE VIEW

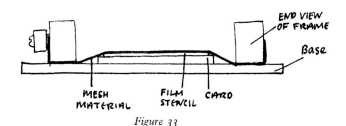

Figure 33

4. All is now ready for the film to be ironed on to the screen. Set the iron to the temperature which is safe for the particular mesh material used for the screen. Iron on top of the newsprint that is inside the frame, keeping the iron moving, Fig. 34.
5. It will be noticed that as the film attaches itself to the screen, it will appear to darken. Continue ironing until there is a uniform dark tone over all the stencil.

*When water-based stencils are to be used it is advisable to de-grease the mesh. This is done by soaking the mesh (silk) with a mild solution of caustic soda for a few minutes. After soaking remove all surplus moisture and with a solution of 33% acetic acid further diluted 25-1, wash the mesh and dry.

6. Lift up the screen and peel off the backing sheet by pulling it slowly away from the screen, Fig. 35. If any of the film

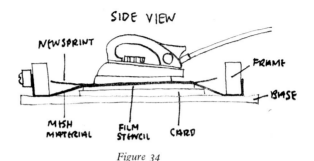

SIDE VIEW

NEWSPRINT

FRAME

BASE

MESH MATERIAL   FILM STENCIL   CARD

Figure 34

begins to pull away with the backing sheet lower the screen and re-iron until it attaches to the screen.

7. When the backing sheet has been completely removed re-iron to make sure that the film has taken to the mesh. Check that there is no open mesh between the edge of the film, and the safety margin, if there is it should be blocked with masking tape. The screen is now ready for printing, see page 41.

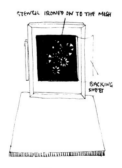

STENCIL IRONED ON TO THE MESH

BACKING SHEET

Figure 35

To Reclaim the Screen. Clean the screen after printing, see cleaning up, page 44. Take the screen from its base, and place a few sheets of newsprint underneath the frame. If Profilm was used pour onto the mesh methylated spirits; with Bluefilm and Greenfilm use warm water. Cover with newsprint. Leave to soak for about 15 minutes. Then remove the newsprint from the top of the screen. Rub the mesh with a piece of rag. Raise the screen, the film should have

28

floated off the mesh and be laying on top of the newsprint underneath. With a clean rag and more solvent give the mesh a final clean. Should any film be difficult to remove, a suede brush used very carefully will clear the mesh.

The use of photographic stencils may be beyond the normal demands of the artist printmaker. Not wishing to become involved too deeply with the technicalities of the photographic stencil, he may not venture further.

However, the stencil method mentioned here is so simple to use that it is worth investigating and perhaps will prove the value of the use of photo-stencils.

Gelatine Dichromate. The stencil method described in this section should be regarded as an introduction to photographic stencils. Gelatine dichromate has been chosen for its simplicity; it is economical to use and suitable for printmaking. However, there are other photographic stencils obtainable from screen suppliers which are just as suitable and in many cases suit particular demands better.

The requirements are that the image to be made into a stencil must be drawn onto a transparent film with opaque paint.

Tracing paper can be used for the transparent film, although its tendency to crease and not be truly transparent makes the purchase of an acetate sheet invaluable. Indian ink although black is not opaque, it is therefore wise to buy opaque paint, photographic retouching paint is ideal.

It will be realized that almost any opaque shape, or mark that can be placed onto the transparent film can be made into a stencil. For example, the film can be painted with a flat area of opaque paint, allowed to dry and then can be drawn into with a sharp point or with wire wool. It is also possible to attach flat opaque objects, leaves, to the film, etc. or use transfer textures, lines or dots.

Summary. The design is painted with opaque paint onto a transparent film, which is then placed in contact with a screen which has been previously coated with a light sensitive solution. The screen is then exposed to light. Where there is no opaque paint the light will reach the solution and harden it, where there is opaque paint the light will not reach the solution and will therefore remain soft. The soft solution is then washed out of the screen, and the hardened solution will remain on the screen as the stencil.

Equipment and materials required:
    Use of a darkroom.
    Light source. The light can be supplied from a light box, this
    can be made quite simply, Fig. 47.
    Transparent film. Opaque paint.
    Measuring jar. Measuring scales.
    Saucepan with lid and basin to fit inside the saucepan.
    Stirring rod.
    Source of heat.
    Wide painting brush.
    Black cloth.
    A wooden board covered with foam rubber to fit inside the
    screen.
    Clock.
    Glass slab.
    Light sensitive solution.
    Gelatine.
    Potassium dichromate.
    Water.

Figure 36

Method of Procedure:
    1. Place the transparent film over the design, Fig. 36, and
    trace the design onto it with opaque paint, that is, paint the
    areas which are to be printed.
    2. Having completed the design the screen has to be sensitised.

To mix the solution. Place two or three inches of water in the saucepan and put onto a low heat, Fig. 37. Measure 20 grams of gelatine,
3 grams of potassium dichromate, 100 cc of water.
    Dissolve the potassium dichromate in the 100 cc of water, mix in
the basin. Add the gelatine. Place the basin containing the mixture

30

PLATE IV. *The Sunflower* by George Todd. It is now possible to obtain a full range of tones and textures with screen printing. These will permit a freedom of expression and a greater versatility. No longer are sharp edges and flat colours the hallmark of the screen print; yet these had limited the early printers to work in almost two dimensions

Figure 37

into the saucepan and heat, Fig. 38. The temperature should not
exceed 75°C. Stir well until all parts are dissolved. Dip the brush

Figure 38

in the solution and apply it to the screen. Each brush stroke should
overlap part of the one before, Fig. 39. The screen should be placed
in the darkroom. The solution becomes sensitive to light when it
has dried and work should be carried out in a safe light.

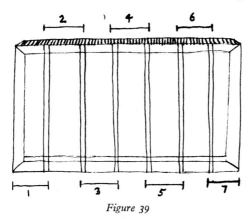

Figure 39

Developing the screen. Place the transparent film with the design drawn on it, upon the light box, paint side uppermost, then place

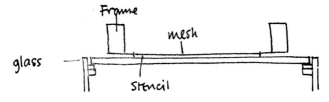

Figure 40

the screen over the top, Fig. 40. Fit inside the screen a black cloth, then a foam covered board, Fig. 41. This will ensure perfect contact between film and mesh and stop straying light. Place a weight

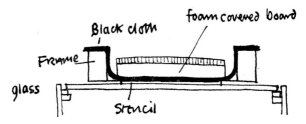

Figure 41

on top of the board, Fig. 42. Switch on the light. The length of time the light is left on depends upon the strength of the light and

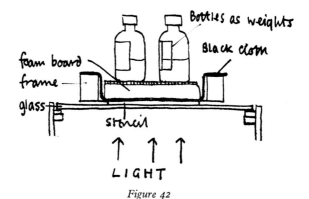

Figure 42

how far it is from the screen. Experiments will have to be carried out to find out the correct exposure time.

32

There is an alternative way to develop the screen without the use of a light box. This can be done by placing the screen over the top of the foam covered board. Lay the transparent film with the design painted on it on the screen and a glass slab laid over the top will give perfect contact, Fig. 46. Expose to the light source which can be the room light, lamplight, sunlight, etc.

Approximate exposure times

150 watts	18 inches away	3 hours.
250 watts	2 feet away	2 to 2½ hours.
3,000 watts	3 feet away	3 minutes.

The exposed gelatine will turn darker than the gelatine which was protected. When the screen has been exposed turn off the light and take the screen off the light box. The screen must be washed down

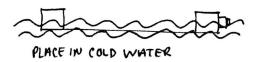

PLACE IN COLD WATER

Figure 43

in cold water for two minutes, Fig. 43. This will stop the unexposed gelatine from hardening as it is taken out of the darkroom into the light. Take the screen out of the darkroom or turn on the room

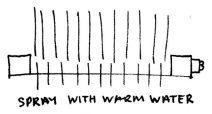

SPRAY WITH WARM WATER

Figure 44

light. Spray the screen with warm water to remove the soft gelatine, Fig. 44. This completed, dry off the screen with newspaper, then leave to dry, Fig. 45.

DRY WITH NEWSPRINT

Figure 45

If a moderate number of prints are to be taken the screen is now ready for printing, but for an edition where hundreds of prints are to be pulled it is wise to strengthen the gelatine. This can be done by covering the inside of the screen with a lacquer, and while this is still wet, the outside of the screen is rubbed with a cloth, pulling the lacquer out of the mesh. Allow time to dry, then paint the outside of the screen, this time rubbing from the inside.

Reclaiming the screen. It is very difficult to remove exposed gelatine dichromate from the mesh. Unless a solvent is specially made to remove it, a new piece of mesh will have to be stretched.

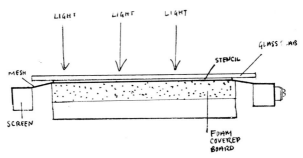

Figure 46

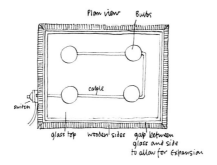

Plan view   Bulbs

cable

switch

glass top   wooden sides   gap between
glass and side
to allow for Expansion

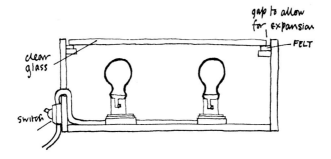

gap to allow
for expansion

FELT

clear
glass

switch

SIDE VIEW

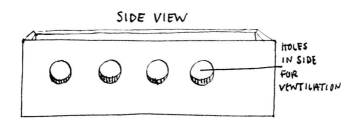

HOLES
IN SIDE
FOR
VENTILATION

Figure 47

CHAPTER THREE

PREPARATION FOR PRINTING

SCREENS AND PRINTING

The number of screens used in producing a full colour print can be limited to one screen for all the stencils, or a screen to each stencil.

Single Screen Method. If only one screen is to be used, this means that each stencil will be destroyed after printing its image. This is inevitable because the screen has to be cleaned and reclaimed in order to apply the next stencil.

It is important to remember this when contemplating printing an edition. It is not until after proofing all the stencils that the image is truly revealed, see printing operation, page 41, and by this time, each stencil will have been demolished.

In order to print an edition with the single screen method a set of duplicate stencils will have to be made, and this is most difficult. Unless, of course, the stencils are very simple, or photographic stencils were used then duplicates can be made; but usually the printmaker has to be satisfied with the various stages of the developing image, and perhaps one or two finished prints.

One Screen to each Stencil. Whenever possible a screen should be used for each stencil, not only does this allow for manipulating the order of printing the stencils, but when the proofs have been taken, the stencils are all still at hand to edition the selected proof.

To operate this method, each screen must be of the same size, with the hinges fixed in a standard position so that the screens can be interchanged easily with the baseboard.

Storage. Storage facilities for screens should not be neglected. A simple rack can be made, to offer the screens protection from damage.

PAPER AND THE PRINT

Paper is the surface where the creation of the image will take place, and is not just a convenient area to accept the print. The ink and paper will become one, with a life and existence of its own. Therefore the selection of paper is no light matter; the paper has to be right for the intended print. Only experience can tell how the paper and print will react to each other, and what qualities will become apparent. The only way the inexperienced can decide which paper will suit which print is by trial and error. Through this, experience will be gained, and also a relationship will begin to be appreciated between the paper and the ink, which was not known before, or even considered. The choice of paper is therefore a matter of personal preference, and each printmaker has his own preferences for particular types and grades of paper. There are literally thousands of types of paper, hand-made or machine-made and all with different characteristics and finishes. It would be a mammoth task and require hundreds of pages to list all papers suitable for printing, giving their specific properties and qualities. I suggest that samples of paper are requested from paper manufacturers and suppliers, and also a p. 63 collection made of as many varieties of paper as possible. It will soon become apparent which papers can be used for rough pulls and which can be used for finished prints. When purchasing paper the most economical way is to buy in bulk, in a quire or a ream, although many quality and hand-made papers are so expensive it is only possible to buy a few sheets at a time.

INKS

It was not so long ago that the silk screen printer would have had to have been something of a chemist in order to produce the colours he needed for printing. For it was not uncommon for many weary hours to be spent in the grinding of his pigments or converting decorators' paint into a consistency which could be squeezed through a mesh.

This, however, is not the case today, printing inks can be purchased from commercial suppliers in such variety that for a printer to be found grinding and mixing his own colours is very rare.

The production of screenprinting inks has now become an exacting science, and long technical explanations and lists of all the various inks would be confusing. I therefore have mentioned the main characteristics of two types of inks, oil-based and cellulose-based.

Oil-based Inks. This ink is cheap to buy in comparison with inks of other bases. It has a high pigment content, and is supplied in an extensive colour range: opaque, gloss or matt finish and can be made transparent. It has usually to be thinned with reducing medium before it can be used. When printing it leaves a relatively thick film of ink. During the printing operation it should not be left for any length of time, for it will begin to dry on the mesh thus clogging it, and is very difficult to remove without damaging the mesh. The solvent for oil-based inks is either turpentine substitute or white spirit. The inks should be stored in air-tight tins, although even

37

when this is done a skin will form on the top of the ink. To prevent this, cover the ink with a layer of turpentine substitute, before sealing and storing.

Cellulose Inks. Cellulose inks are relatively expensive to buy; and can be used almost straight from the tin. They are supplied opaque in a wide range of colours, and can be made transparent or dry semi-matt. When printed they leave a thinner film than oil-based inks, and have a good coverage capacity and dry quickly: if left on the screen for a short period they tend not to clog the mesh. Shellac or plastic laid stencils will be attacked by cellulose inks and should not be used. Cellulose ink requires special thinners and cleaners. This along with the ink produces a strong smell, which is regarded as its main disadvantage. The inks should be stored in air-tight tins and do not form a skin.

Oil and cellulose inks should not be mixed together. Between them they can satisfy demands of the printmaker. It is always wise to buy good quality inks. Inks in the cheap price range are given to inconsistency of mix, and fading of the colours. If old inks are used, then it is best to sieve them through a piece of spare mesh material. This will remove any foreign bodies or lumps.

Colour Mixing. There is a wide range of colours available, and these are as paint is to the painter, having to be mixed to produce the correct colours needed. Each printmaker has his own way of arriving at which colours are to be used; either through the working out of the layout, see The Image, page 17, or through experiments during printing, see page 46. Once they have been decided upon they have to be mixed. This can be done in the following manner.

Materials Required:
    A selection of inks and transparent base.
    Storage tins with lids.
    Push knife.
    Rag.
    Solvent and ink thinner.
    Sample of printing paper.
    Glass slab.
    Newsprint.

Procedure for mixing colour. Lay the glass slab on top of a sheet of white paper. This will enable the colours to be seen against the white. Open the tins of ink which you think will be needed for the mixing of the colour. Place small amounts of ink on top of the glass

77

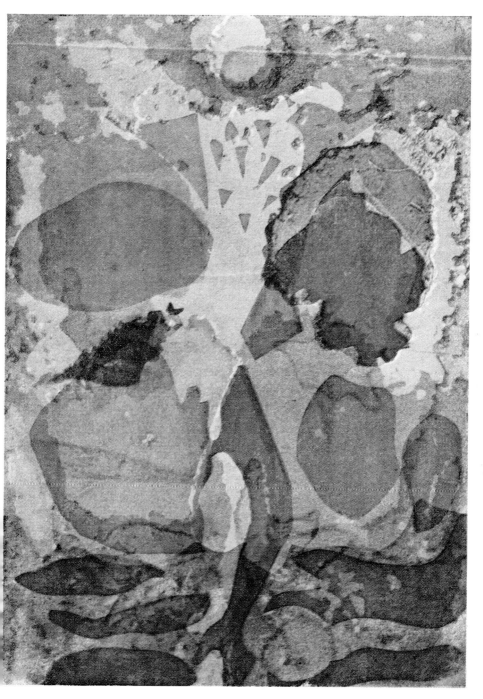

PLATE V   *Children Bathing* by Bert Humphries.   When two transparent colours
are overlapped one over the other, a third colour will naturally be created.   Further
overlapping will increase the combination in which new colours can be formed.
The above print shows a very sensitive and successful use of transparent colours

slab, wiping the push knife clean each time the ink is taken from a different tin, Fig. 48. By taking scoops of ink from the top of the

glass slab and mixing them together in the centre, the colour needed can be mixed, Fig. 49. Mixing must be carried out as quickly as possible, for most inks contain dryers. By taking a sample of ink

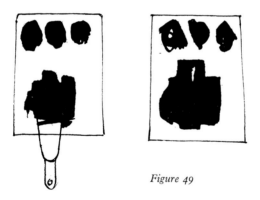

Figure 49

at various stages of the mixing then dabbing it on to a piece of the printing paper, it is possible to see the true value of the colour. When a satisfactory colour has been arrived at, it will be necessary to mix up a quantity of colour to enable an edition to be printed. The amount of ink required depends upon how many prints are to be made, and even when that is known there is no rule of thumb. Only through experience can the printmaker truly judge the correct amount. It is always better to mix up too much than have to mix up a second batch as it is nearly impossible to produce exactly the same colour.

Colours can be made transparent by the use of a transparent base mixed in with the ink. It is simply mixed by adding the ink to the

F

base, until the required strength is achieved.

The use of transparent colour will produce a second colour each time it is overprinted. The ink should be mixed so that it runs smoothly and fairly quickly off the push knife.

If the addition is only small, then the ink can be left on the glass slab, but for large editions it should be transferred to a tin with an air-tight lid, and taken out as it is required.

Note. It is a good idea to dab a sample of ink on to a piece of card and tape it to the ink tin so that the true value of the colour can be easily seen.

REGISTER OF PRINTS

Two pieces of information are required in order to secure good registration. To know where the image will fall when it is printed; and where to position the paper to be printed, so that it can receive the image in its required position.

Registration of the first colour. The most versatile form of registration I have experienced, to answer these questions, is by manipulation. This is achieved by placing a sheet of newsprint, the same size of the paper to be printed, upon the printing area; and by lowering and raising the screen (with the stencil attached) and by adjusting the newsprint, it is possible to decide the most suitable position for the image to be printed. This achieved, the newsprint is registered at the corners by marking the printing area with masking tape, Fig. 50.

REGISTERING THE NEWSPRINT

FIRST PRINT ON NEWSPRINT

Figure 50   *Figure 51*

Lower the screen and take a print, Fig. 51, this will verify that the position is correct. Remove the newsprint and continue to print the first colour of the prints, see printing operation, page 41.

After printing, the screen has to be cleaned, see cleaning up, page 44. If one screen is being used to print all the images, the stencil will have to be removed and the screen reclaimed; then the stencil for the second colour is attached. In the case where a number

40

of screens are being used, the screen with the stencil to print the second colour is attached to the baseboard.

The second colour. Place the newsprint with the first colour on it onto the register marks and tape it temporarily to the baseboard, then lay a sheet of tracing paper over the top and attach it also to the baseboard, Fig. 52. Take a print. If the second colour falls in the

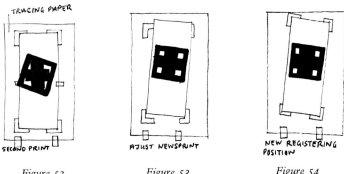

| Figure 52 | Figure 53 | Figure 54 |

correct position on the tracing paper in relation to the first colour then the register marks can be used again, but if it does not, then move the newsprint, which is under the tracing paper, to the position where the first colour registers up with second on the tracing paper, Fig. 53. Mark at the corners of the newsprint in its new position and remove the old registration marks, Fig. 54. Take away the tracing paper and the newsprint. Register the printing paper up to the new marks and print the second colour.

This procedure should be followed for each subsequent colour.

THE PRINTING OPERATION

Proofing. The printing of the stencil is the climax to all the preparation in which so much time and energy has been engaged.

The stencil will at last be made to reveal its exact visual content: colours to be printed will become meaningful and the birth of the image will have begun. This transition from the stencil to the growth of the image is generally termed as proofing.

The growth of the image usually continues until all the proofs have been made, making modifications, and establishing colour and stencil relationships. It is quite possible that from all the proofs made the artist will have a great variation of images, and perhaps only one print considered complete.

41

If the single screen method is to be used, it may not be possible to make reprints of the completed print, see screens and printing, page 36.

Before printing commences, all the materials and equipment to be used in the operation has to be inspected, this is to find any discrepancies which can cause trouble later.

Inspect

1. That the screen is attached correctly to the baseboard, no movement caused by loose hinges, etc., and also that the screen can rise, and be lowered, see baseboard, page 9.

2. The mesh should be completely clear of any blockage in the open areas where ink is intended to pass.

3. Check the soundness of the stencil used.

4. The squeegee must be in good condition and the blade free from nicks.

It is important that the printmaker be well organised. Materials should be close at hand, ready for the printing operation.

1. Paper for printing to be placed near the screen, see paper and the print, page 36.

2. Colour to be printed, also near the screen, see mixing ink, page 38.

3. Drying racks nearby, see drying racks, page 72.

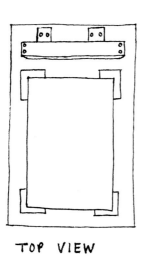

TOP VIEW

Figure 55

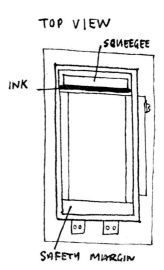

Figure 56

Printing procedure. The first print will be a trial run.

1. Place a sheet of newsprint, the same size as the printing paper, on the printing area, and place register marks at the corners, Fig. 55, see registration, page 40.
2. Lower the screen.
3. When the ink is thoroughly mixed or prepared, place a small amount on the safety margin at the top of the screen.

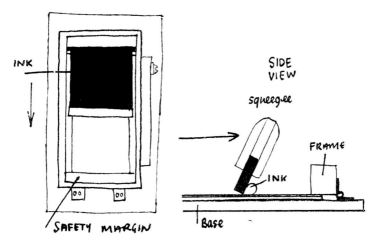

INK

SIDE VIEW

squeegee

FRAME

INK

SAFETY MARGIN

Base

Figure 57

4. Take the squeegee and place it as in Fig. 56. Hold it with both hands at an angle of 45°, then pull it firmly across to the other side of the screen, Fig. 57 and 58. The squeegee should bite the mesh as it is pulled across, forcing the ink through the open areas with a scraping action. The ink and the squeegee should always be brought to rest at the hinged end of the screen. To make a second pull, scoop up the ink with a squeegee, Fig. 59, and place it at the top of the screen and repeat the action.
5. The screen has to be raised; to stop the squeegee falling over, a simple device can be fitted, Fig. 60.
6. Lift up the screen. Take hold of the top two corners of the newsprint and pull away from the screen, Fig. 61. If the print is faulty, see faults in printing, page 46.
7. Having pulled a satisfactory proof and the stencil is sound, all is ready to make a set of prints. Place a sheet of printing paper on the printing area, registering up to the marks. Lower the screen and print.

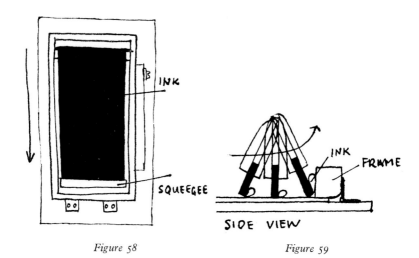

TOP VIEW

INK

SQUEEGEE

INK FRAME

SIDE VIEW

Figure 58   *Figure 59*

8. Work at a steady and constant speed, this will prevent the ink drying on the mesh.

9. Take care that the prints are kept separate while they are still wet. See drying racks, page 55.

CLEANING UP

Immediately after printing, the job of cleaning up has to be undertaken. This is not a pleasant task, although it is most vital to the welfare of the printing unit. The following is a guide to solvents and their applications.

To be removed	*Solvent*
Oil-based inks	Turpentine substitute, paraffin, white spirit
Water-based glue	Warm water
Water-based stencil	Warm water
Cellulose inks	Special cellulose solvent
Shellac	Methylated spirits
Lithographer's ink and greasy crayon	Turpentine substitute, paraffin, white spirit

44

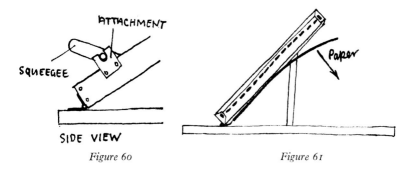

SQUEEGEE

ATTACHMENT

SIDE VIEW

Paper

Figure 60   Figure 61

Procedure

1. The first consideration should be for the screen. Any surplus ink around the edges should be removed. If the ink was mixed, it is wise to store the remainder in an air-tight lid; ink that was used straight out of the tin and is still in good condition should be returned. See inks, page 37.

2. Take the screen from the base and place it on sheets of newsprint. Pour solvent on the screen, enough to cover the

NEWSPRINT
BASEBOARD

Figure 62

mesh, Fig. 62. While this is soaking, clean the squeegee and push knife with the solvent, using a piece of rag. If a paper stencil was used it should be removed from the underside of the screen.

3. With the screen laid on the newsprint gently rub over the mesh with a rag, pushing the ink through the mesh onto the newsprint underneath. It will be necessary to remove the top layers of newsprint and change the rag as they become saturated with ink and solvent. Add clean solvent to the screen as it is needed. Lift up the screen and clean the underside of the mesh. Ink should be removed from the corners of the frame. By lifting the screen up to the light it is easy to see if any ink remains in the mesh.

4. The stencil will still be on the screen, and if it is not wanted, will have to be removed. To do this, check that the screen is perfectly dry, and free from any remaining ink.

45

5. Place clean newspaper under the screen and with a rag, add the solvent which will remove the stencil, and let it soak for a while. If water is the solvent this operation should be carried out in a large sink.

6. When the mesh is entirely free of the stencil, hold the screen up to the light and check that it is completely clear. Dry the screen and return it to its base.

FAULTS IN PRINTING

The word fault in this section should be interpreted to mean 'an unwanted occurrence'. Thus defined it is possible that if a fault is wanted and can be integrated in part of a print it is no longer a fault. Many printmakers purposely create 'faults' in order to use the qualities produced; in fact some faults are so regularly used that they almost merit becoming standard procedure.

It would almost be impossible to mention all the faults which occur in printing, due to endless combinations in which they can be produced. Many faults can be discovered before the printing operation begins, and when a fault is found, the solution is usually self evident, and can be corrected. If the cause to the fault is also known it should be noted to prevent recurrence; the cause is usually revealed by methodically back checking every past action.

The list below is of a dual purpose, it is a guide to the prevention of faults by knowing how they can occur; and the action to take after they have happened.

Faults which can occur in printing with paper stencils, film stencils, or hand painted stencils:

Fault: Unwanted ink leaking through onto the print, Fig. 63

Cause: Fault in the stencil or in the safety margin.
Solution: Clean ink away from the leaking area, and block out the mesh with a water-based glue.

Fault: Gradual disintegration of the prints, Fig. 64

Cause A: Stencil breaking up.
     B: Clogging of the mesh.
Solution: Cause A. Clean all the ink off the mesh, and repair the stencil. If the stencil is beyond repair reclaim the mesh and apply a duplicate stencil.
            Cause B. Clean all the ink off and out of the mesh, allow to dry; check the consistency of the ink and continue printing.

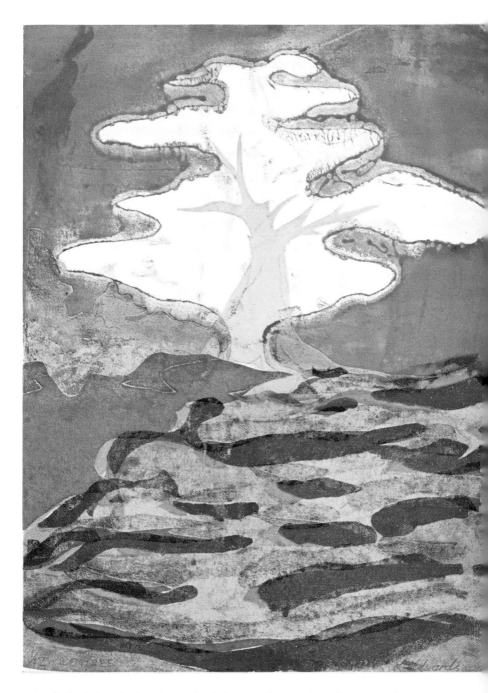

PLATE VI. *The Ice Tree* by Lee Edwards. Many printmakers purposely create 'faults' in order to use the qualities produced. The present print is an excellent example of how 'faults' may be effectively and successfully integrated as part of the print

Figure 63

Figure 64

Figure 65

Figure 66

Figure 67

Fault: Colour or tonal streaks

Cause: Ink not completely mixed.
Solution: Clean the screen, and remix the ink, thoroughly blending and mixing the colours.

Fault: Misprint or white streak, Fig. 65, 66

Cause A: Insufficient ink for the squeegee to pull across the screen.
       B: Gritty substance being pulled along with the ink.
       C: Nick in squeegee rubber.
Solution: Cause A. Add more ink to the safety margin.
            Cause B. It is wise to remove all ink from the screen and clean the mesh; clean the squeegee, and inspect that no grit is in the ink supply.
            Cause C. Sand down the squeegee rubber on the sanding block until the nick is removed.

Fault: Parts of the print merge with the imprinted areas, Fig. 67

Cause: Solvent remaining in the mesh and being squeezed through with the ink.
Solution: Clean the screen and thoroughly dry the mesh with a clean cloth.

Faults which can occur when using gelatine dichromate:

Figure 68

Figure 69

Fault: Small dots of ink coming through the gelatine stencil, Fig. 68

Cause A: Badly mixed sensitising solution.

     B: Air bubbles in the solution when it was applied to the mesh.

     C: Solution not correctly applied to the mesh.

     D: Grease on the mesh when the solution was applied.

Solution: Causes A, B, C and D. Clean the screen. If the small dots of ink are only slight, they can be blocked out with a water-based glue. Intensive 'pin hole' grouping may make the repair of the stencil almost impossible, if this is the case it is better to make another stencil.

Fault: After exposure, the solution washes out of the mesh

Cause A: Solution heated over 75°C.

     B: Under exposed.

Solution: Causes A and B. Wash out all the gelatine dichromate from the mesh, and prepare the stencil again.

Fault: Loss of definition, Fig. 69

Cause A: Solution applied too thickly to the mesh.

     B: Negative not in perfect contact with the screen during exposure to the light.

Solution: Causes A and B. Nothing can be done; remake the stencil.

Fig. 70 shows the print free from faults.

Figure 70

High temperature and humidity can affect the solution and the printing, therefore a normal temperature should be maintained in the workroom.

The printmaker should not be too dismayed when printing begins to go wrong. Out of so-called 'bad prints' can come a whole range of images which should not be discarded. He should keep himself flexible and not be too fixed and rigid in pursuing his original ideas.

THE EDITION

To produce an edition is no easy task, it requires physical effort, preparation, organisation and the ability to master any technical or mechanical problems which may arise during various operations.

Once the proofs have been taken to their logical conclusions and no further statements can be made, the creative part is now finished. Preparation has to be made for printing the image.

The number of prints in an edition depends upon the intended use for the prints. An edition of about thirty prints will suffice for the personal use of the artist exhibiting; loaning, selling, etc. A larger edition of a minimum of 70—80 must be printed if the edition is to be sold to a professional print dealer. Each print must be identical, with no variations between prints. Margins around the print must be clean and not damaged in any way. If these demands prove too much then it is possible to have the edition printed by dedicated craftsmen who specialise in the printing of artists' work.

Upon deciding to print your own edition the workroom has to be streamlined to deal with this task. The whole printing operation must be organised from start to finish, from the registering of the printing paper to the hanging to dry of the wet print, see printing operation, page 41. To operate the printing of a large edition by oneself can be extremely exhausting. The help of a friend in the placing to dry of wet prints etc., can be almost essential.

DRYING RACKS

The wet print is taken from under the screen: it may only be a first colour, it could even be a bad print, or perhaps it is the very last colour to be applied. Whatever stage or state the print is in, it must be handled with great care. Never will the print be in a more vulnerable state than it is now; I have known some printmakers to be inadequately equipped at this crucial moment, with nowhere to put the wet print!

Figure 71

The problem is how to keep each print separate from each other, and safe until they are dry enough to be stored. One quick temporary answer, for large prints, is to string a line arrangement across the

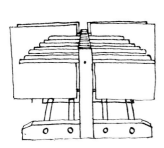
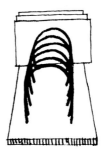

Figure 72

79 studio, and hang each print up with a clip-on-peg, Fig. 71. A more permanent answer, for prints, printed upon card can be found in the simple rack arrangements, Fig. 72, where the cards are stood in a simple rack arrangement.

Some printmakers allow themselves to be without a drying rack, but the majority are found to be well equipped, and some prove themselves to possess great ingenuity in the designing and building of an apparatus to hold their valuable prints while they dry. This is an absolute must for the serious screen printer.

CHAPTER FOUR

THE FINISHED PRINT

The printing is finished, everything has been cleaned up and stored, and the prints are hanging in the drying racks: the ink and paper both lifeless when they were lying separate in the studio, now have a life of their own.

The artist should accept a responsibility towards his prints, always handling them with respect.

The Selection. When the prints are dry and taken from the drying racks, the edition has to be selected, see the edition, page 54. How printmakers select their prints to make up the edition varies. Personally I clear a large area upon the studio floor and lay down sheets of newsprint. The prints are then placed evenly upon the newsprint; if it is not practical to find room for them all, lay the remainder aside for a moment.

Any prints which are damaged, torn, creased, etc., will have to be rejected, and removed from the floor; being replaced by the prints laid aside. Prints are also removed if they have any faults: bad register, smudged colours, etc., see faults, page 46, or any differences as to deviate from the body of the edition. The number of prints which usually are rejected is about 10%. This figure can be a lot higher especially if an edition is printed for the first time.

The Signing of Prints. Once the prints for the edition have been selected, each one has to be recorded and signed.

Before I actually sign the prints I select a print which I consider to represent the best state of all the prints and store it with my personal collection. I advise the reader also to do this, for it is possible for an edition to be sold out, and the artist can be left without any prints from that edition. A collection of all the prints will be invaluable in revealing the artist's development to himself.

The practice of signing prints is carried out in the following manner. With a pencil and directly beneath the bottom of the print the artist signs his name in the right hand corner, the title is placed in the centre, and in the left hand corner the number* of the print is

*Each print is given an individual number from the first print No. 1 to the last print, each print being marked consecutively. This is purely for record and in most cases does not relate to the order in which the prints are printed.

recorded, along with the total number of the edition, for example, print No. 1 of an edition of 100, should be marked 1/100.

The rejects from the edition, and the proofs used in the development of the image can also be signed, the artist's signature being applied in the usual way; immediately beneath the bottom of the print in the right hand corner; but to the left of the signature is written "Artist's Proof". All other prints not wanted should be destroyed.

Care of Prints. The care of finished prints is of the utmost importance; the damage of prints through negligence or accident lessens the edition and in most cases cannot be afforded.

Ideally prints should be kept flat, never be rolled, for the ink will be in danger of cracking and the paper bruised. With the handling of prints care must be exercised, sets of prints should be transported horizontal upon stiff board, and when carrying single prints use two hands.

Professional printmakers usually have storage cabinets in which they can keep their finished prints. These cabinets consist of a set of shallow sliding drawers, allowing a drawer for each edition. The price of one of these cabinets may prove to be too expensive to purchase during the initial outlay and many printmakers use a set of imperial size folders. If possible the folders should be stored flat; standing them upon their edge often produces creased prints, caused by the prints sliding downwards and bending.

A Reference of Prints. It is a simple matter to check upon the whereabouts of one or two prints, but as more editions are printed the number of prints leaving the studio will be considerable; being exhibited, loaned or sold, etc. Because of this it is most advisable to keep a record of each print. This is done by recording, preferably in a ruled book, all the details of the edition, for example, date of printing, title, number of colours, etc., and then list the number of each print in the edition. Information of sales, location, etc., can be recorded against each print, every time one is despatched from the studio.

Presentation. When a print is to be exhibited, some thought has to be given to presentation. What constitutes good presentation differs between artists, and there is no rule of thumb which can be applied.

Traditionally prints are mounted with card, set with the card away from the edge of the print, leaving a margin between the print and the mount. The placing of a mount around a print is done basically to isolate the print from its surroundings so that it can be viewed without distraction. The print can be presented simply in a mount, or framed and glazed.

Card can be purchased in many colours and various tones. When selecting card for a mount, care should be taken that it will not command too much attention when placed around the print; a plain white card or light tone is generally used.

Once the card has been chosen, it has to be cut to accept the print.

To Cut a Mount. Before beginning to cut a mount, the workroom has to be organised. Cleanliness is essential and newsprint should be laid upon the working surface, hands should be washed.

Materials required:
    Sheet of mounting card.
    Print to be mounted.
    Metal rule.
    Sharp cutting knife.
    Adhesive tape.
    A rubber.
    Pencil.
    Brown paper.

The mount is cut from a sheet of card measuring about 4 inches larger from each side of the printed image, although this is subject to preference. An area slightly larger than that of the image area is cut from the centre of the card, thus making a frame. The card is then placed over the top of the print, displaying the image through the removed area. The print is then attached to the mount.

Method of Procedure:

   1. The size of the image is measured, adding $\frac{1}{2}$ inch to an inch to each dimension, this allows for the margin between the card and the print.

   2. It has now to be decided where to cut the area of card through which the print will be displayed (referred to as the window). I find that by cutting a piece of brown paper to the measurements of the image area, and placing it upon the card, it can be moved into a suitable position. As a guide, there should be slightly more margin at the bottom of the mount than at the top, in order to make the print look central; and the margin of both sides of the mount to be slightly narrower than that of the top.

3. When the brown paper is in position, mark a dot at the corners with a sharp pencil. Remove the paper from the card and with a rule join up each dot. The card is now ready to be cut.

4. Place several sheets of newsprint where the card is to be cut, this will protect the working surface from knife cuts, and the knife will not be easily blunted.

5. Lay the metal rule along one of the pencil lines; the rule should be laid upon the margin, this will protect the mount if the knife slips. With a sharp knife, and firm pressure holding the metal rule in position, cut at an angle of $45°$ along the line, taking care not to pass the corners.

6. When the side of the window has been cut, (look underneath the card to inspect that the cut is all the way through) move to each side in turn, cutting through the card along the marked lines.

7. This complete, the centre of the window should, in theory, drop out, but in practice it is usually held by uncut pieces of card deep in each corner; attend to the corners and tap out the centre.

8. With the mount complete, lay it over the print and place in position.

9. The print has now to be attached to the mount, this is done by carefully sliding print and mount slightly over the edge of the working surface. From this position pieces of tape can be placed under the mount, temporarily attaching the print. The mount is then turned over, and the print is fixed securely.

10. The mount can be finished off by attaching a sheet of paper to the back, an inch or two smaller than the mount. Inspect that the face of the mount has no pencil lines or dirty marks upon it, if there are, they can be removed by erasing lightly with a rubber.

Frames. The framing of prints enter a little too far into personal preference to give any detailed advice. The function of the frame is much the same as that of a card mount, although being more permanent, and if glass is used, will be protective to the print.

Correct lighting conditions must exist for prints framed with glass, bad light reflection can make the viewing of the print almost impossible.

Reproduced below is a part of the *Definition of an Original Print:* issued by the International Congress of Artists in Vienna, 1960, which the artist printmaker may find useful.

1. It is the exclusive right of the artist to fix the definitive number of each of his graphic works in the different techniques: Engraving, Lithography, Woodcuts, etc.
2. Each print, in order to be considered an original, must bear not only the signature of the artist, but also an indication of the total edition and the serial number of the print.
3. Once the edition has been made, it is desirable that the original plate, stone, wood block, or whatever material was used in pulling the print edition, should be defaced or should bear a distinctive mark indicating that the edition has been completed.
4. The above principles apply to graphic works which can be considered originals, that is to say to prints for which the artist made the original plate, cut the wood block, worked on the stone or on any other material. Works which do not fulfil these conditions must be considered 'reproductions'.
5. For reproductions no regulations are possible. However, it is desirable that reproductions should be acknowledged as such, and so distinguished beyond question from original graphic work. This is particularly so when reproductions are of such outstanding quality that the artist, wishing to acknowledge the work materially executed by the printer, feels justified in signing them.

THE WORKROOM AND MATERIALS

The choice of a workroom depends entirely upon individual preference and what facility is available. Basic requirements are a reasonable amount of space, plenty of natural light, ventilation and running water. It is not practical to give a set layout of a workroom, but for a guide see Fig. 73.   83, 84

The beauty of screen printing lies in its simplicity and also the fact that only a small capital outlay is required before a full colour print can be produced. It would be a mistake to interpret this to mean that the process can be efficiently and successfully operated 'on a shoe string' or by 'making do'. To be well organised and reasonably well equipped is always sound practice.

I have entered below the names and addresses of suppliers from which can be obtained almost everything required by the screen-

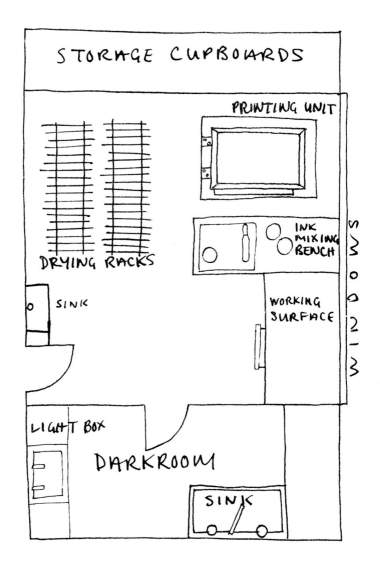

Figure 73

printer. Materials are usually acquired gradually, and as most printmakers have limited funds, the basic essentials being obtained first then added to.

Screen printing materials

Screen Process Supplies Ltd., 24 Parsons Green Lane, London, S.W.6.

George Hall (Sales) Ltd., Beauchamp Street, Shaw Heath, Stockport.

Selectasine Silk Screens Ltd., 22 Bulstrode Street, London, W.1.

Dane & Co. Ltd., 1 Sugar House Lane, London, E.15.

Treleaven & Son Ltd., 108 St. James Street, Liverpool, 1.

Avdance Process Supply Co., 2315 W. Huron Street, Chicago, Ill., U.S.A.

Atlas Silk Screen Supply Co., 1733 N. Milwaukee Avenue, Chicago, Ill., U.S.A.

Devoe & Raynolds Co., 787 United Nations Plaza, New York, U.S.A.

Process Supply Co., 313 Hanley Industrial Park, St. Louis, Miss., U.S.A.

Sherwin-Williams Co., 260 Madison Avenue, New York, U.S.A.

Ulano Products Co. Inc., 610 Dean Street, Brooklyn 38, New York, U.S.A.

Paper—hand made

J. Barcham Green Ltd., Hayle Mill, Maidstone, Kent.

Paper—hand and machine made

T. N. Lawrence & Son Ltd., 2/4 Bleeding Heart Yard, Greville Street, London, E.C.1.

Paper—machine made

Spicers (Merchandising) Ltd., 8 Julian Road, Sheffield, 9.

74. The frame: with the aid of a piece of string the frame will be held in position

75. *The frame: having decided which mesh is to be used, it has to be stretched over the frame*

76. *The frame: finishing off the job by removing all rough edges with a medium sandpaper*

77. *The printing operation: materials should be close at hand ready for the printing operation*

78. *Colour mixing: although there is wide range of colours available, they are as paint to the painter—having to be mixed to produce the exact colour needed*

79. *The drying rack: it is essential that there is somewhere to put the wet prints*

80. *The aim of this book is to present the medium of screen printing to the artist, to reveal the potential, and to show fully what the medium can offer*

81—82. Revealing the potential of the medium

83. The workroom: storage of frames and baseboards

84. The workroom: storage of frames and baseboards

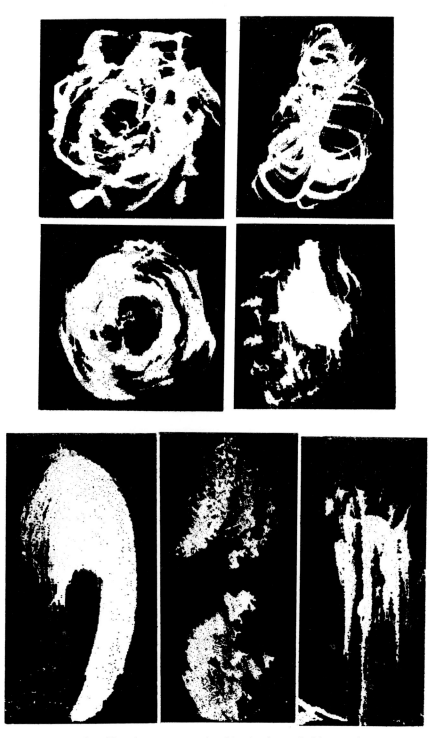

85. Negative textures produced by the glue method (page 21)

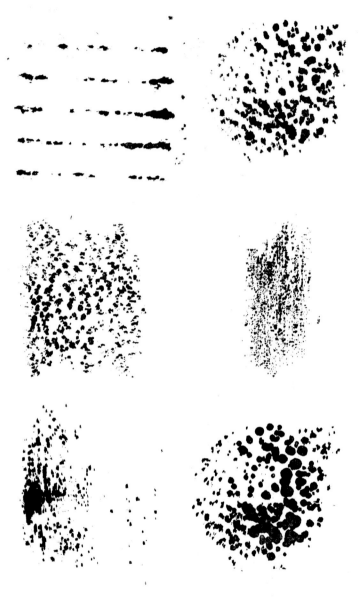

86. Examples produced by the grease method (page 24)

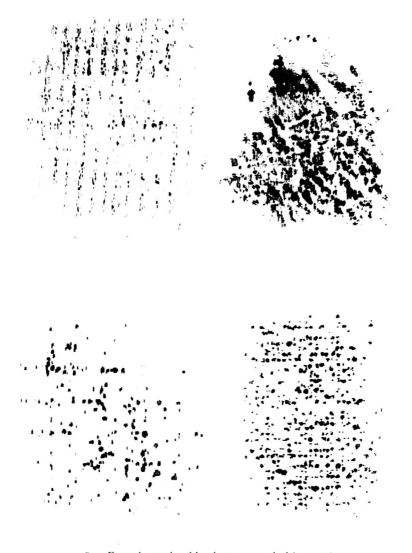

87. Examples produced by the grease method (page 24)

(FIGURES 86 AND 87 SHOW THAT THIS METHOD WILL RENDER A WIDE RANGE OF TONES,
AND ALLOW SCOPE FOR TAKING RUBBINGS DIRECTLY ONTO THE MESH)

88. This was the first proof taken from a photographic stencil (gelatine dichromate page 29)

77